DISCARDED

Date: 4/11/11

AC-130H/U GUNSHIPS

BY CARLOS ALVAREZ

BELLWETHER MEDIA · MINNEAPOLIS, MN

TM

Are you ready to take it to the extreme?
Torque books thrust you into the action-packed
world of sports, vehicles, and adventure. These books
may include dirt, smoke, fire, and dangerous stunts.
WARNING: read at your own risk.

Library of Congress Cataloging-in-Publication Data

Alvarez, Carlos, 1968-
 AC-130H/U gunships / by Carlos Alvarez.
    p. cm. – (Torque: Military machines)
 Includes bibliographical references and index.
 Summary: "Amazing photography accompanies engaging information about AC-130H/U Gunships. The
 combination of high-interest subject matter and light text is intended for students in grades 3 through
 7"–Provided by publisher.
 ISBN 978-1-60014-493-6 (hardcover : alk. paper)
 1. Spectre (Gunship)–Juvenile literature. 2. Gunships (Military aircraft)–United States–Juvenile
 literature. I. Title.
 UG1242.G85A45 2010
 623.74'6–dc22   2010000866

This edition first published in 2011 by Bellwether Media, Inc.

The images in this book are reproduced through the courtesy of: Ted Carlson/Fotodynamics, pp. 12-13;
all other photos courtesy of the United States Department of Defense.

Printed in the United States of America, North Mankato, MN.
010111   1183

CONTENTS

THE AC-130H/U IN ACTION

Wind blows across the desert. United States soldiers move toward an enemy base. The enemy knows they are coming. Enemy trucks carry machine guns into position. These guns are aimed at the U.S. soldiers. Suddenly, an AC-130 flies overhead.

The AC-130 opens fire before
the enemy can react. Enemy trucks
explode. Enemy soldiers run for
cover. Their defenses have been
destroyed. The U.S. soldiers have a
clear path. The gunship heads back
to base. Its **mission** is a success.

GROUND-ATTACK AIRCRAFT

The AC-130 is a ground-attack aircraft. It is a huge airplane loaded with powerful guns. It flies low and slow. It protects and assists U.S. soldiers on the ground. This is called **close air support**.

The Air Force stations its AC-130U models at Hurlburt Field in Florida. The AC-130H models are stationed at Cannon Air Force Base in New Mexico.

U.S. gunships destroyed more than 10,000 enemy trucks during the Vietnam War.

AC-130H Spectre

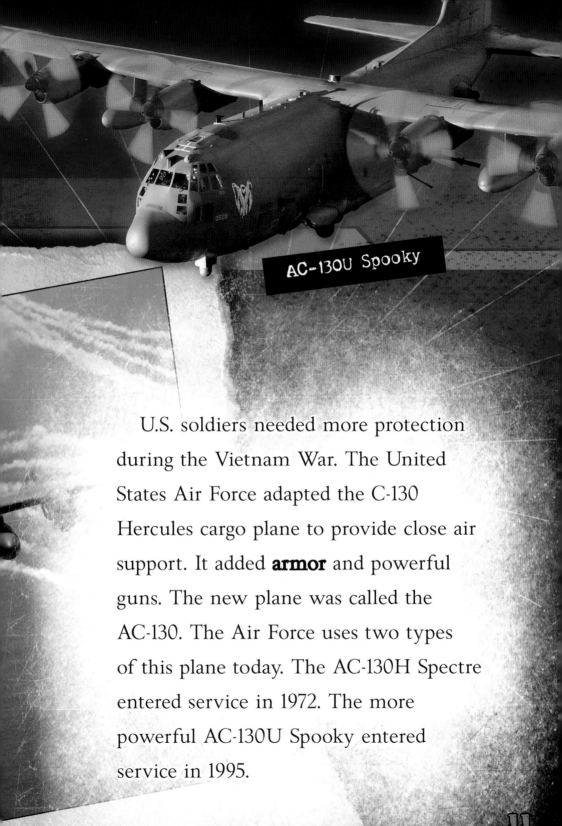

AC-130U Spooky

U.S. soldiers needed more protection during the Vietnam War. The United States Air Force adapted the C-130 Hercules cargo plane to provide close air support. It added **armor** and powerful guns. The new plane was called the AC-130. The Air Force uses two types of this plane today. The AC-130H Spectre entered service in 1972. The more powerful AC-130U Spooky entered service in 1995.

WEAPONS
AND FEATURES

The AC-130 is designed to fight. It stays close to battles. That makes it a big target. The AC-130 needs a lot of protection. Its armor helps protect it from enemy fire. It also has equipment that can jam **radar**.

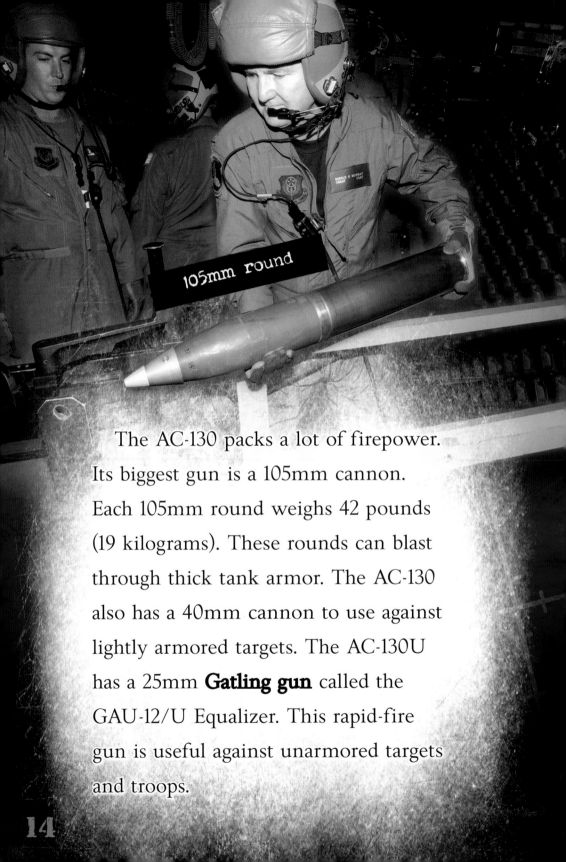

105mm round

The AC-130 packs a lot of firepower. Its biggest gun is a 105mm cannon. Each 105mm round weighs 42 pounds (19 kilograms). These rounds can blast through thick tank armor. The AC-130 also has a 40mm cannon to use against lightly armored targets. The AC-130U has a 25mm **Gatling gun** called the GAU-12/U Equalizer. This rapid-fire gun is useful against unarmored targets and troops.

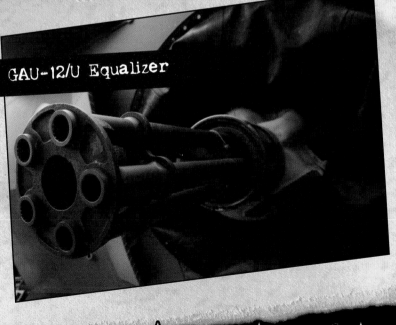

40mm cannon

105mm cannon

GAU-12/U Equalizer

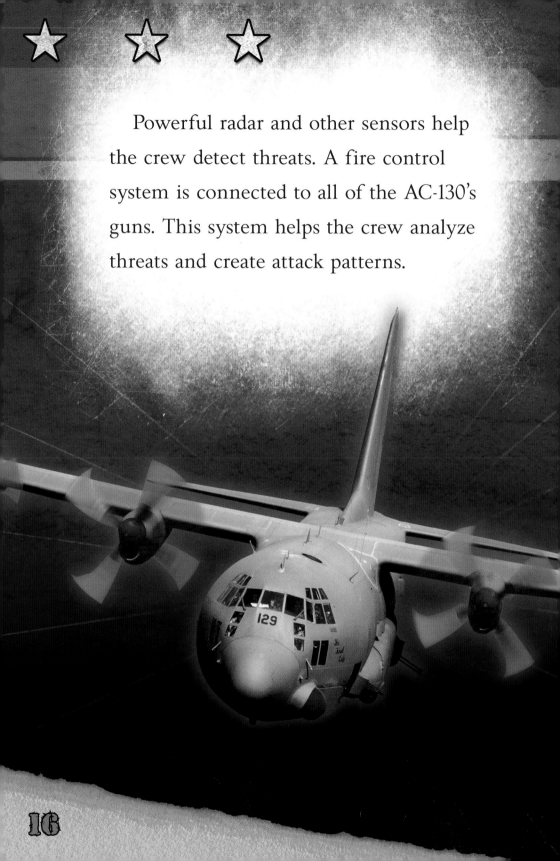

Powerful radar and other sensors help the crew detect threats. A fire control system is connected to all of the AC-130's guns. This system helps the crew analyze threats and create attack patterns.

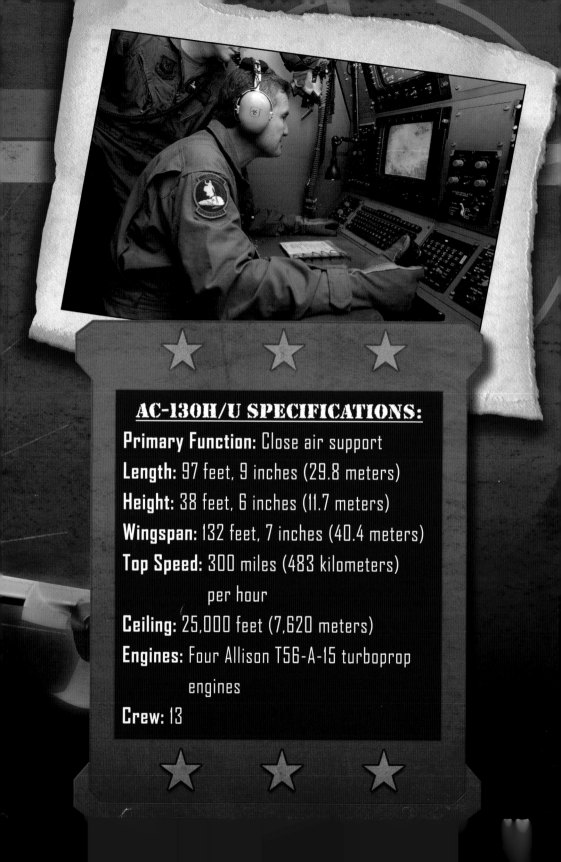

AC-130H/U SPECIFICATIONS:

Primary Function: Close air support

Length: 97 feet, 9 inches (29.8 meters)

Height: 38 feet, 6 inches (11.7 meters)

Wingspan: 132 feet, 7 inches (40.4 meters)

Top Speed: 300 miles (483 kilometers) per hour

Ceiling: 25,000 feet (7,620 meters)

Engines: Four Allison T56-A-15 turboprop engines

Crew: 13

AC-130H/U MISSIONS

The AC-130 is used only by the U.S. Air Force Special Operations Command. The Air Force uses the AC-130 to provide close air support to soldiers on the ground. The AC-130 also provides protection to U.S. bases. Many of the AC-130's missions happen at night. Enemies have trouble seeing the plane in the dark. The plane often goes in a tight circle around the enemy. Its guns stay aimed on the target as it fires.

An AC-130 can use countermeasures to stay safe. Countermeasures confuse enemy missiles so they do not hit the AC-130.

A crew of 13 operates an AC-130. The pilot and co-pilot fly the plane. A **navigator** helps them. Four **aerial gunners** control the weapons. The other crew members operate the plane's electronics and sensors.

The AC-130 is a powerful force in the air. For U.S. soldiers, there is no sight more welcome than an AC-130 swooping in to save the day.

pilot

aerial gunners

21

GLOSSARY

aerial gunners–crew members who operate the AC-130's powerful guns

armor–protective plating

close air support–the role of supporting and protecting ground troops against enemy forces; close air support is the primary mission of the AC-130.

Gatling gun–a machine gun that has multiple barrels on a rotating frame

mission–a military task

navigator–the crew member in charge of assisting the pilot with directions and helping plot a course

radar–a sensor system that uses radio waves to locate objects in the air

TO LEARN MORE

AT THE LIBRARY

Fitzpatrick, Kevin J. *Flying Gunship: The AC-130 Spectre*. New York, N.Y.: Children's Press, 2000.

Roberts, Jeremy. *U.S. Air Force Special Operations*. Minneapolis, Minn.: Lerner Publications, 2005.

Zobel, Derek. *United States Air Force*. Minneapolis, Minn.: Bellwether Media, 2008.

ON THE WEB

Learning more about military machines is as easy as 1, 2, 3.

1. Go to www.factsurfer.com.

2. Enter "military machines" into the search box.

3. Click the "Surf" button and you will see a list of related Web sites.

With factsurfer.com, finding more information is just a click away.

INDEX